Hamlet Off Stage

D. C. Berry

Texas Review Press
Huntsville, Texas

811
B533h

FIRST EDITION, 2009
Requests for permission to reproduce material from this work
should be sent to:

    Permissions
    Texas Review Press
    English Department
    Sam Houston State University
    Huntsville, TX 77341-2146

Cover graphic by Dan Dew. Cover design by Paul Ruffin

Library of Congress Cataloging-in-Publication Data

Berry, David Chapman, 1942-
  Hamlet off stage / D.C. Berry.
    p. cm.
  ISBN-13: 978-1-933896-30-4 (pbk. : alk. paper)
  ISBN-10: 1-933896-30-2 (pbk. : alk. paper)
 1. Hamlet (Legendary character)--Poetry. 2. Shakespeare,
William, 1564-1616--Characters--Poetry. I. Shakespeare,
William, 1564-1616. Hamlet. II. Title.
  PS3552.E745H36 2009
  811'.54--dc22
                              2008054022

DATE DUE

Elgin Community College Library
Elgin, IL 60123

FOR JOHN MARTIN, MARK LUMPKIN,
KYLE THORNHILL, AND VIRGIL BRAWLEY.
ALL FUN PROVOCATEURS

CONTENTS

SKULL LUNCH PAIL —1

HAMBO RAMBO—2

BLONDE DITTOS—3

MEL GIBSON'S MOVIE OF ME—4

PANSY ICELANDIA AND PANTY TOAST—5

GQ's MAN OF THE YEAR—6

SUCKA HOORAH—7

THE MARDI GRAS AQUARIUM ACTIVITIES—8

RADISH ME MAMA—9

SNAIL, THE PSYCHIATRIC SLIDER—10

OPHELIA APPALACHIA—11

BOOBS GERTRUDE—12

THE GOOSE, MY IDOL—13

THE ART SHOW LAWDY MAMAS—14

LAERTES PUNKS ELVIS—15

FORTINBRAS MIGHT SET HIS TAIL ON FIRE—16

HAMBEAU LE FRENCH—17

MAY NOT MONSIEUR SERPENT THINK POSITIVE—18

FACES, SIDEBURNS, AND BALLS—19

MADAME HAMLETTA DE POMPADOUR'S PARLOR—20

HAMBEAU HEADBROKE AND HORNY—21

DADA NICHT MAMA LAMA DALI—22

BEAUTY PARLOR PSYCHIATRY—23

PIGGY AND PUFF DADDY—24

POLONIUS VIAGARASAURUS—25

MONTY BRINGS OUT THE MAMA IN THEM—26

HAMBONE TWO TONGUE DOUBLE TIMING—27

MISS OPHELIA COSMOTOLOGIA—28

CHOLLY FOLLY BEACH—29

THREE RACCOONS STEP OUT—30

THE TURTLE PEANUT BUTTER & JELLY—31

WEEDEATER BUZZMOUTH—32

DON'T COUNTRY THIS HEE HAW—33

TAI CHI SPIDER PARLOR—34

SERGEANT DEATH WON'T BE SERIOUS—35

FATHERS' DAY WITH CLAUDIUS—36

SWISS REVENGE ULTIMATES THE DREAM—37

HAMLET STICKS HIS NOSE IN HIS BUSINESS—38

ST. OH—39

SOMETHING'S ROTTEN IN NORTON'S ANTHOLOGY—40

OPHELIA AND GERTRUDE BIKINI THE POOL—41

QUEEN BARBIE AND KING KEN—42

REYNALDO LOSES HIS MARBLES—43

HE HORTICULTURE SONG—44

PRINCESS DIANA AND OPHELIA VICTORIOUS—45

GERTRUDE NEVER WITHOUT A TAMALE LONG—46

THREE-LEGGED GOD—47

OPHELIA'S CHI OMEGA OVER-ALLS—48

SWEET NOTHINGS—49

GERTRUDE'S CIRCUS TAIL—50

CAN NAVY BOY DO IT—51

MOTHER LOVE GONE COUNTRY—52

PIRATE FOO FOO—53

HAMBOO AND THE OEDIPUS COMPLEX APARTMENTS—54

YOURS, LOVE FOREVER DROOL—55

LET MR. J. ALFRED PRUFROCK BE A LESSON—56

THE ICEMAN HERE AND THERE THE PANTYBLITZ—57

HAMLET TIGHTENS UP THE MLA—58

LAERTES ATE A PELICAN—59

THE PLAY'S SWEET 400TH—60

OH QUEENLY TO THE LAKE—61

CHRISTMAS SHOPPING EASY—62

SKULL TURTLES INTERRUPTUS—63

OPHELIA SWANS HER LADYSHIP—64

NEW YEAR'S EVE AT THE TIT FOR TAT—65

ZEN WART—66

FORTINBONE AND HAMBONE XYLOPHONE—67

FORTINBRAS FROM AIR FORCE ONE, FIRST SOLILOQUY—68

SKULL LUNCH PAIL

I loathe this play much as I loathe myself:
black clothes, the graveyard shift, the skull lunch-pail.
Nobody's who he is. Who acts like Who.
God's blood. The play's a toilet of questions.
Flush one, another splashes in your face.
The play's first two words shout, "Who's there?"
Good Dr. Freud? Or Dr. Fraud?
Or Who? I'm psychiatric bait without a hook.
Some nights can't catch a ride after the play.
Me with my empty skull lunch pail. Taxis
just tap the brakes and stare like full hearses:
Sorry, you don't look dead enough, call at midnight.
I yell, "Help your local ventriloquists" and flash
the skull. They squeal off like they think the skull
is the ventriloquist and I—Hambo—the doll.

HAMBO RAMBO

I ought to be at World Wrestling College,
tackling the craft of Vengeance Theatrics,
honing my Elvis snarls and Hitler sulks,
at least learning to cheat at solitaire.
But can't. Too mother-fuddled. Mom's a cow,
a sex freaknoid, a forked trap door—where's mom?
I've heard her Moo. Why do moms keep humping?
Squeeze out a kid, I say, then kiss goodbye
the bedroom coos and sorority war whoops.
I'm born. What but the grunt in mom craves more
mounting? By Claudius? By Claude His Balls.
Kill him, I Hambo will. I Hambeau Sissy shall
with Hambaud's poems fright him to death: Hamboo!
Hambone him till he gags his soup. Except,
Hollywood waits, wants me to play Hamlet.
Go? Or coax Claude to Gulfport for roulette?
The arrow click on his number, I'll know
the UFO was dad, no devil blowing smoke…
Claude bull, I matador will prick his soul
till by his weight he splashes on my sword.
His blood will be the cape by which I trump
him, which should chill mother's love of the hump.

BLONDE DITTOS

I fall in love with two blonds in tight jeans
ahead of me. I catch up and they are—
yank my greasy toupee—they are the girls:
Ophelia and Gertrude, my black-root blondes,
Oh Puke Me and Mon Mom, the Barbie babes.
The two so one, one's ribs the other's harp,
and Claude busy plucking the strings of both.
I won't touch Oh. I'm into deep hygiene.
I'm clean of the whole Maybelline coven.
This boy pounds his baton like Beethoven.

MEL GIBSON'S MOVIE OF ME

Mel Gibson's Hamlet, that's doll Mel. Wind up
Mel, and Mel's eyes melt into bluebird milk,
blue pools of earnestness, and blue Gertrude
sucks it all up, swills Mel's sincerity—
the jokeless Mel, Mel Duh, Mel Doll. Mel knows
a joke's loose only when cued by the laugh
track, Gertrude in his lap, slapping her knee,
making me want to screech my do-die speech
about the dew: dissolve into adieu—
adieu, a dew, a do-die dodo you.
The closest dad ever came to a dew
was when, pell mell into the flames, he yelled
adieu/a dew—a joke lost on doll Mel,
Mel outplayed by even ye olde castle.

PANSY ICELANDIA AND PANTY TOAST

We're on the coast—Spring Break—bronzing our buffs,
toning Budweiser abs, and our butt-string
yummies sun-tanning their yoyos. But what?
Icelandic cold, ice-cube eyes, I'm depressed.
I got the blues, the pansies got the blues,
bleached in their shiny strait-jackets of frost.
No quandary to our hiney-thonged Gertrude,
out baking panty toast with jet-ski bums,
her buns burning and freezing hot, cold, hot,
in this do-or-die world in which you bid
a grave and call a wedding. Life's a piece
of cake, but wedding cakes are sugared urns.
Give me pansies and their frozen faces.
They wear death as cool as Claudius slides
a wedding band on his dead brother's bride.

GQ's MAN OF THE YEAR

Back on the beach, Ophelia and I sweat.
Beer foams. Throngs of college-tail tan.
But I am deeply slumped in black flip-flops.
My smile is black, leer black, lips black-on-black.
But you'd crack your bald egg picking which me
is me from all my clones, all my frat clowns
dressed aping me, spruce in their black Speedos,
black panty caps, black towels. We smolder
like Nazis under black umbrella skies.
But I feel cheer as Herr Fashion Fuhrer.
These KA's think I'm Denmark's heir. These dumbs
forget heirs get their hair parted with swords.
But what the hell, rock-steady lads,
my brave boys—up, courage! They, hoist their beers
and cheer me as GQ's Man of the Year.

SUCKA HOORAH

This play's a sham, a fake, a faux, a scam,
horse pie, cow pie, a rat, a ruse, a hoax.
First guys on stage all but shout THRILLER PLAY:
Bernardo, Francisco, and Marcellus . . .
spaghettioso names that pledge blood sauce
right now, like over at the rival stage,
where bulls gore bears to fill bloodthirsty seats,
and no talky-talky foreplay, no spit-lather
before some shitass gets his neck shaved off.
Our Bill wants his hands on that bloody purse.
So, on our stage, before you've warmed your seat,
in glides the ghost and says, Pray, spill the King's
blood, now! Had I, Hamlet would have been called
Hambo, Blood Mafia Revenge.
But does blood flow, here? Nay. Bill serves you words,
play words, plague words, apple-sauce words, and drone,
act after act of poetic chewing the fat
before you got an old rat leaking blood.
Hypocrisy, humbug, horse plop, faux, hoax—
our Hamlet is Shaky Bill's Judas kiss:
blood on his lips, but dry words on his tongue
for hours one, and two, and three, and you
all puckered up for blood. You paid to get
your guts pulled out, and Shaky pulls your leg.

THE MARDI GRAS AQUARIUM ACTIVITIES

There in the French Quarter at Mardi Gras,
some soused Germans kept yelling smut at Oh,
"O Feel You, O Feel Me, flash us der nips."
She flashed the bird, while her granny gown dripped,
and her snake necklace sipped the air. I wore
a jock and juggled armadillo skulls.
Some skinheads heckled me to use der jock
as a slingshot to shoot skulls at der friend,
"Das oogly skinhet dare, nuck his noose off.
C'mun Hambo. Actung, Hamboscovitch,
do it, Heil Ham." I spent most of my day
diving for Oh, who in cement-block boots
was tip-toeing through the aquarium's bottom,
her snake gasping, while she twiddled her thumbs
as might a paddle-wheeling submarine.
She twiddles at the shrink's. At the aquarium
made sense. But at the shrink's, looks dumb.

RADISH ME MAMA

Mother's a bitch in heat humping to please
most any wagging boner ambling by,
flops on her back and offers her radish,
while dad plays ghost and tells me to play God—
to kill Claude and to start Eden over:
recycle tabloids into toilet rolls,
starve mothers of their sex fantasies. How?
How when there's always that radish,
and we love dirt like a head of cabbage?

SNAIL, THE PSYCHIATRIC SLIDER

For better brain hygiene, nothing can beat
the Snail Mobile Clinic. He slides to you
fast as his paving foot allows, his white
hard hat on should an icy curve race up.
It's in his patience, you will find healing.
But some say his patience isn't patience,
say he's a sissy-boy riding the brakes,
befuddled. No. He's prudent. Slow because
he paves his road in case he must return
to me, fallen back in my black toilet
of questions: wear cap backwards or forwards?
Or to the side? And which way bend the brim?
And where's forward when I should run backward
and lop the head I should have lopped off yesterday?
Yes, Dr. snail, do pave your primrose path.
And could I squeeze into your hat,
I'd know which way to march.
I find your prudence Roman as an arch.

OPHELIA APPALACHIA

My Miss Oh baby-hugs a mandolin
and caterwauls she wants my baby bad,
makes up rude tunes, and wails-out wildcat screech,
hard-jaw, bloody, Kentucky-gothic blues,
like she's a cat strangling nine toms at once.
She shames me, calls me Prince Hambone No Bone
because I won't climb in her family tree.
Too many crotches in a family tree.
Too many crutches there to break my legs.
Tuff titty. Oh squalls mama-kitty tears,
but I'm a tom won't risk torn ears.

BOOBS GERTRUDE

Crack houses whisper Claudius has AIDS.
Tell Mom? Or let her croak of AIDS with him?
Her all floozied-up like a sex side-show:
fake claws, tongue stud, and silver nose bugger.
Also the Corps of Engineers boob job
shows she's bound for the Padded Cell Motel:
her breasts perky sandbags, but no river
flooding, while she drowns in any mirror.

THE GOOSE, MY IDOL

At dawn I soldiered strong at Shotgun Pond,
goose hunting—honka honk. Five birds splashed down.
I held my fire. Here's what I think they honked:
"Yes, I like corn, honk. Do you like corn? Honk
honk. I like swans, too. Yes, I do like swans."
One honked, "Boys, honk honk, I'm ready to live."
I whispered, "Wish I shared your pagan view.
It beats the Baptist: live ready to die."
The Shotgun Pond Symposium. What they
told me was Beep before you fly backwards.
But Beep as whom? Abercrombie or Fitch?
Hambo or Hambeau? Which me can I trust?
The geese trusted nothing. Their necks hula'd
like cobras in mongoose land. Weren't goofy,
but floated snake-faced in their goosefulness.
I'll imitate their careful carelessness.
Or, should I say their careless carefulness?
But till I think clearheaded as a goose,
I shall play my cards like a closet Zeus.

THE ART SHOW LAWDY MAMAS

If you're a rose hog, here you'll grunt, Oink oink.
Got roses, roses, and unrare roses.
Most life-like, though many more like road-kill.
Ophelia had five real ones in her hair.
From one she'd squirt what smelled like lemonade.
Doused people glanced about like startled cats.
A spry antique granddame, old as Gertrude,
said she'd like to show me her flowerbed
of barbed-wire pansies and bullwhip jasmine,
her tongue a poetry rocket flaming out.
I gassed her up with purple punch and left.
Back to pick-up Ophelia. Picture this:
she'd ripped herself a handful of roses
from several paintings. She promised me they
were real red boys and never would fade brown.
I thought about my gray gynopoet,
who'd wanted to show me her barbed-wire bed.
One crazy femme, same as Ophelia, but
I'll take Ophelia. Each day she's sweeter,
though wilder and wilder. Talks of climbing
the willow at the creek, straddling a crotch,
and letting God pick her like a forget-me-not.

LAERTES PUNKS ELVIS

Dumb Laertes, the dunce and dull dummy,
Laertes, he now thinks he is invisible.
He can't so much as yawn without screaming,
"Yo, look at me. I'm here, right here, right here."
And, now, he's punked his hair with purple spikes.
Rhino resemblance, true, popsicle horns,
but where is Laertes? Our Laertease
remains invisible as an icon,
like Mary back in the Middle Ages,
the pin-up who, since she hung everywhere,
nobody saw, was multiples of nought.
Where art thou, Laertes, popsicle prick?
He forms a band, puts five Laerteses
on stage with him, all with their hair yanked by
the cosmetish at None In Hell Snow Cones.
They call the band E Funk, their Elvis snarls
identical. Seen none, you've seen them all.

FORTINBRAS MIGHT SET HIS TAIL ON FIRE

Fortinbras part-times as a pro wrestler,
the Neon Savage, jackass of jive-ass..
His clothing line also Neon Savage.
Thinks he came up with wearing baseball caps
backwards, patent pending as male jewelry.
Gets backwards forwards left and right mixed up,
eyes blinking like competing turn signals.
Not knowing which way to steer or not steer,
but he kneels to his uncle's gold advice:
"For Denmark's crown, all you need is patience.
Denmark is now a sewer of self-hate,
which by the weight of its own stink will flush
itself; then, you'll be king and so gracious
you'll bury Hamlet as Hambo, Soldier,
but on his box print Joker, or else you'll
confuse the Devil. But here he's Soldier.
Here all knees bow to hypocrisy; thus,
paint Ham bloody with your bullshit airbrush."

HAMBEAU LE FRENCH

My razor-thin mustache and saber puns,
notice. Notice, I sit in Pascal's chair
and let dear friends come knocking down my door.
Forget jall that UFO folderol
out in Aztec, New Mexico. Why search
for dad passing the pipe with freaks I'll sit
in Pascal's chair and watch hip hop TV,
where rappers jabber and arrest themselves,
jerking like traffic cops on puppet strings.
Why leave the house when weird's a flick away?
Dad wouldn't know me as Hambeau l'Pompadour
and gobbledegooking my double talk.
He'd yell, "Where's, Hambo, my young man?" I'd squeak,
"Pray, here, Claude's liver on my breath!" Pun talk:
Claudius has a liver, and he is
a liver, too. I Hambo am Hambeau,
am noble, but no bull, yet full of bull.
A wag, perhaps. Sir, your poodle.

MAY NOT MONSIEUR SERPENT THINK POSITIVE

I must think positive now I'm Hambeau
Le Smile, must curl my lips even at snakes.
Think positive and Sneaky Pete smiles back,
even extends to you the pink handshake,
and that's most neighborly, considering
he must breast-stroke armless to crawl about.
His fangs fine, too, the Pearly Gates for rats.
Think positive. Fangs are the serpent's crown,
first Satan's horns, then thorns passed on to Christ.
Think positive, therein salvation lies,
the cross a plus-sign that life does add up.
Even our sneaky snake thinks positive.
When lightning cracks, he curls into a ring,
a bride enters, and soon they trade rattles.
I, Hambeau, will comport myself likewise,
will curve minus-signs into Buddha smiles
and eat bananas for their golden curve.
Claude will think positive that I'm no snake,
that I've no more backbone than a necklace.
But my fangs are its clasp. Handle With Care.

FACES, SIDEBURNS, AND BALLS

Teen creeps, my table almost touches theirs—
courtier kids: pre-fab ripped jeans, riot hair,
braces they show off like Rolls Royce chrome work,
their French-kisses wrecks waiting to happen.
Back when I was a creep, braces meant red faces:
"What happened, Snot, you eat a ball of wire?"
Thus rattled Golden Balls and Rosy Crotch,
our fashion chemists, first of us to bleach
the hair and show us water-bomb condoms
to throw at girls and set their screams on fire.
These boys debuted our first Mohawk haircuts,
our firsts with Corvettes, tops down, A/C up.
They think they'll run me down and crack my head,
collect my thoughts, and read them like tea leaves.
What they don't know is what my boxers know: my
sideburns grow down to my B1 Bomber balls;
I'll blow these cuckoos so high they won't fall.

MADAME HAMLETTA DE POMPADOUR'S PARLOR

Our play is mostly lame psycho disco,
a circle-jerk sick jazz of double-talk.
Our shrink, Doc Nosy. Doc's a toy cannon
we spin around like a roulette arrow
and bray our junkyard lives at its black hole.
It may blow smoke back or blast a fortune
cookie reply like, Go Ask Nat King Cole,
or Arsenic Martini For Mortal Sip,
or Please Padlock Your Mother's Panties, Please.
Round and around, we gab at Doc Nosy.
Gertrude weep-talks like she's got Oprah's ear.
Mom says, "How'd I get pregnant on my honeymoon?
Nay, from the night's first grunt, his birth
has never been more than the squirt that hurts."

HAMBEAU HEADBROKE AND HORNY

Ophelia cuts our love into confetti bits
easy as scissors say, Snick Snick.
I try to crawl out of my throat and yell,
"You can't," but can't, my tongue's a donkey merde.
Life smells. I'm rot, dead of a broken head.
We don't think with our hearts, but with questions:
How part my hair? How part the day from night?
The only white I see are Oh's panties. I creep away, all
boxed up in my stealth—
head broke, balls aching, but in perfect health.

DADA NICHT MAMA LAMA DALI

I like a cow, her nose a fruit doorbell.
Ring it, her tail goes strolling like a cane.
That's poetry, the kind my father penned,
given to puns, as he lived in two worlds.
But mom pretends the world is prose. Take tails:
tell her a snake is two tails, her eyes cross.
She says, "The snakes I see are all one-tailed."
But what's a missing tail to my mother?
A tail's a tail: lose one, grab another,
you'll find one hanging on most any guy.
Her mind's Old Testament—eye for an eye.
Her soul Germanic—*dis ist dis, nien das.*
I'm French, and words my milk, my tongue's a teat.
If you hear turkey talk, that's mein mutter,
Hear Moo, that's me unswelling my utter.

BEAUTY PARLOR PSYCHIATRY

For discount psychiatrics, Oh and I
like beauty shoppes. Your hair's your crown,
your thinking cap! Fresh hair, fresh mousse, fresh life.
Your hair's also your personal ad. It tells
us who you are and what your eyes peeled for.
Hair short, you think you head's a bowling ball
into Republicans in flashy silky shirts.
Worn long, then you're a hair evangelist
hoping to meet a blonde wooly mammoth.
Some beauty parlors Oh and I like are:
Our Hair Won't Scare, Wig Bomb, Hair Here and There,
and Coleman del Pierre's Doggy-N-Style.
For problems only ritzy rinses fix,
like boring sex, first try Razzzl Dazzzl
Head Shoppe . . . restores any wild hair that's out
of kink. Insomniacs like Curl & Dye. Nazi
baldies like Doctors Wig Toupee & Nails.
I find myself at Love Ahem & Her Hairem.
Your head feel upside-down, see your stylist.
Confident Hair Your Best Psychiatrist.

PIGGY AND PUFF DADDY

The spirits of our dead parents live in our dogs.
The spirits of our ex's in our cats.
Take my Basset, Piggy. He slobbers mother love.
Whether I'm fat or gaunt, I'm his Hambone.
While Puff, my tom, is crazy, vexed by love
gone off the rail. In his screechings, I hear Oh cry
like she's been sleeping on a tack too long.
Tom weeps, but also tries to find where life
went off track: takes off like a spinning wheel,
ears pinned back, and races around the room,
bouncing off couch, TV, chairs, and the walls—
Puff, he's our black emergency eyeball
chasing a thread of meaning for us all.

POLONIUS VIAGRASAURUS

Polonius, old twat, takes Viagra,
the high-sap pill that stiffens timber rot,
which his splinter most marvelously needs
if it's as limber as his flapping tongue.
Viagra, to what end? Who slip it to?
Left hand or right? No doubt he flatters both,
as I do. And that's not the only way
we mirror each other. We're both critics,
actors, agents, directors, and scribblers,
stage cods for whom the curtain never drops.
Talk is once he was Gertrude's evening star,
and I the son that rose out of their sheets,
making Miss Oh my half sister. Maybe
that's why he won't let us trade valentines,
to save us from rowing in incest's ditch.
There's no telling how wisely he's cuckoo.
Only acts like a mole when in the sun,
while I bury my head like an ostrich.
When he scratches, I itch.

MONTY BRINGS OUT THE MAMA IN THEM

Miss Oh Feel and I saw The Full Monty,
a film of naked slobs with dongs flopping
like dead rodents. The women whooped and howled
like they'd never seen mice minus their tails.
Question. These gals cheer these men as he-men
or litter runts needing a mother's love?
Perhaps applauded them as both: right hand
clapping he-men, left clapping litter runts.
How do they clap for opposites at once?
Let me explain: all women are Gertrudes,
paws out, ready to pounce on any mouse
of shy spirit and down to his left hand.
Women will give you their right hand or left.
Each female's Jezebel in red silk thong,
each Mary in Egyptian white drawers.
God saw Eve's eye would want both these colors
and built the first Victoria's Secrets,
only to fold, as Eve preferred fig leaves.
Even for God, women are too complex.
You buy her white panties, she wanted red.
Get red she says, "I wanted white. It's you like red."

HAMBONE TWO TONGUE DOUBLE TIMING

I'm big of tongue, but don't have any ears.
I tell the clowns don't throw in extra jokes,
then I don't listen to even myself.
I skip and jape with any ass on stage.
And I can't act. My black clothes can. Kidding.
Want action? I'm your Muzak action ape.
Kill Claude? No, but I'll poison Father Time
with jazz while passing gas at either end.
But cant kill Claudius. Have slain on stage
so much I'm too ho-hum to spill real red.
Too trite, the clenched-jaw rant and epic fist.
No. I'm kidding. If you'll but wind my tail,
I'll be your big-mouth Hulk and yell and growl
like there's a bulldog clamped down on my lip.
I'll crush the King. Armed with my poesy,
I'll strangle that whoreson with my red thong
and snip his balls off, throw them to you pigs
for pain…to hear you Oink. Let's everybody yawn.
My words more gilt on Claudius' crown.
But, you know, then, you know, ad-libbing skits
beats playing father's most unChristian script.

MISS OPHELIA COSMOLOGIA

Those days when I'm cold dead and life's a crow,
Oh says, "Your outlook hangs on how you look,"
and unsnaps her cosmetic carnival:
got tubs o'love, creams, eyebombs, tints, and rouge.
She buffs and dabs me till I disco glow.
Rabbits mistake me for an Easter egg.
When life is too bright for my chicken skin,
Oh screens me with Tuscany Potion Six,
or with Sun Block Fascia SPF 19,
maybe Day Glo Health Skin with SPF 15,
or VO5 Hot Oil Treatments with Oats 18.
Week-day facials, quickee Kleenex wipe-offs.
But on weekends, she cakes me with Marvin's
Freeze Dried Protein Yam Lip and Laugh Line Peel
or Andrea Eye Q's No Stress Eye Mask.
Thanks to Miss Oh I have a pretty face.
But am I just another pretty face?
Another rotten egg wearing make-up?
My pretty head's a pretty bongo, but
will any rabbit's foot thump me good luck?

CHOLLY FOLLY BEACH

We bronze, and ski, and kite, and bobby-q.
Baroque's my thing, shells maniac-spiraled
like those that twist in God's own can of worms,
two such maggots—my old friends R&G.
And I'm a bottle of black sour wine
their corkscrew tongues twist to uncork my thoughts.
 "Hambeau, you sporting Porsche sunglasses, dude?
Why wear them upside down? For hotter cool?
And, dude, your Danish double dap handshake?
What? Like a white guy polishing the air."
So say detectives RG Dumb & Dumb.
They think the world is their apple,
and I'm the worm they'll unravel.

THREE RACCOONS STEP OUT

I'm clipping my toenails, again, and one
looks like a small golden potato chip,
a sign my hand's not lost its Midas touch,
then three raccoons march by in single file,
tails tall, and high heels on too tight.
They haven't lost their touch for gold, either,
so many rings on, make a rapper swoon.
They're rich, also, in raccoon honesty,
as testified by their Lone Ranger masks.
For unlike Claudius—who'll steal a crown
and hide behind asses and whereasses—
raccoons are too righteous to drop their masks.

THE TURTLE PEANUT BUTTER & JELLY

My hands shake like bongo fever. Relax,
I tell myself, you worry wart, you noise.
Act wise. Take an 18th-Century view of life;
uncork your ass from that poot-jar and act
enlightened. Act smart, if you can't be smart.
"Act smart, and smartness will be unto you,"
as found in Ye Turtle Boke of Ye Revelate.
How act enlightened? Act like a turtle,
who turns to gold any grief he's given:
his belly doesn't drag, it's his skateboard;
his shell, the Pearly Gates through which he glides;
tumped on his back, four hands hitch-hiking rides.
Ophelia has such a turtle philosopher,
who's either double puzzled, has two heads,
thus two names, Peanut Butter & Jelly,
or he's double enlightened, sees both sides
of fake smilers, same as Ophelia does,
and lets it go, life's a two-lane banana peel.
Miss Oh never complains about fake smiles—
they are the peels on which everyone slides.

WEEDEATER BUZZMOUTH

I hate the weed eater's hemorrhoidic roar,
its hyper-manic, wailing, high-pitched whine—
yeow yeow yeow yee pop pop pfhop.
Laertes is one of these weed lightweights.
And wears no muffler, so he draws all eyes.
Nobody hogs applause more in this play
than Larry Mouth, as in Ophelia's grave,
his hard-on that he loves her more than I,
him all slobber, foamy pro-rasslin rant.
But not because Oh Kill Me lies there cold.
He yeows because I yeow as well as he . . .
his clutch slipping KA WHACK, mine slapping WOCK.
I'm not above a prank
and pull his leg to hear him crank.

DON'T COUNTRY THIS HEE HAW

Though some find my mustache a face fungus,
I'm not into nature. Bugs piss me off.
Nature's too out-doorsy, too bitchy-French.
So, when I cut the grass, I'm all Nazi
blitzblade, skinning the lawn putting-green flat.
Yet, once showered and shaved, ich bin le Beau
Hambeau, again—parfumed, perfumed, and preened,
once more Ophelia's poetry pantyman.
I splice with nature about like Rousseau.
I'll toot the flute out on the lake, then scram
inside before Miss Oh misses her one-man band.
This week she's Cosmo's Nature Girl Celeb:
fig eyes, apricot blush, and kiwi tan.
Miss O's as close to nature as I get.
For us landscape fuehrers,
a Country Club is quite Hee Haw enough;
plus, that thousand-legger under my nose.

TAI CHI SPIDER PARLOR

I'm studying Tai Chi, learning to creep
like spiders and most gently trip the King—
under-do it like sex in Christian porn,
like flames do strip-teasing for their shadows.
I do not pinch God's nose. I spin my web,
while Claude Balls and Gertrude go ape on ape,
wrecking and thumping into walls. Who sleeps?
I get up and sleep-waltz, do my tai chi
dumb show and dream of how to make Gertrude
see her Humpty Dumpty's a rotten egg.
I've cracked her mirror so she sees herself.
Now, slip behind it, silent as a black
widow, and spin the hole in place through which
Claude's balls will drop into hell's blaze (surprise),
cut loose by God, and me no more to blame
than a shadow slow-dancing with its flame.

SERGEANT DEATH WON'T BE SERIOUS

I spray-painted the barn Halloween White,
it guaranteed to scare mildew away,
and got white-washed myself. Looked like a ghost.
The wind to thank, which made the ladder sway
like at a suicide-polka party,
with Sgt. Death asking, "Ham, this our waltz?"
I washed-up and went to a funeral,
old flame of mine who'd married Sgt. Death,
toward whom I'm still a virgin, though will wink.
My flame had crawled into the box with him,
and there she lay, threatening to smile, her face
as sugared as a wedding cake.
But I don't trust Sgt. Death. Once he's got
your pumpkin grin, he blows your candle out.

FATHERS' DAY WITH CLAUDIUS

We went to watch two world champeens rassle—
the Easter Egg versus Hell's Own Lite Bub.
A rabbit rolled the Egg into the ring,
where Lite Bub tip-toed, prancing and bubbling.
These mugs high-stepped in circles and heckled
exactly as Laertes and I do;
sometimes yelling solos, sometimes duets.
"They're frauds," said Claudius. I saw actors,
rant-schoolers like the Edward Alleyn troupe,
who thunder squall and clutch their cods and glare—
apocalypse one night, the next Armageddon.
I cheered for Egg and his murder conscience.
Claude, backed by John Locke, said, "Style's but skin deep."
I, backed by David Hume, said, "Style's brain deep."
We butted heads awhile, then Claudius
said, "Son, you're right," and I said, "Dad, you're right":
us fraud parrots, working reverse psychology.
I like the faux-biz of the stage and ring,
both perfect worlds: pure fake, no irony.
I take Claude under my arm and say, "Claude,
maybe no one's a fraud—we're all diamonds,
and fraud is only one of our facets.
All of us eggs playing omelet's.

SWISS REVENGE ULTIMATES THE DREAM

I find Claude Clown down on his knees, praying,
and I can glacier-slow slaughter his ass
seventeen ways with my Swiss Army knife.
First, twist the can opener and pop his eyes
open, so he'll see we're in no cartoon.
And then screw down his tongue, no interviews.
And leather-punch any late word balloons.
And grab the pliers, double grip, and pull
the bloody rug from under his red eyes.
Then out the corkscrew and uncork his ears.
We'll let him catch his breath. He'll hear the breeze.
But think its champagne hissing when he screams.
When I flip out the blade, he'll think he dreams.

HAMLET STICKS HIS NOSE IN HIS BUSINESS

I stabbed that busy bitch Polonius
and killed myself. Mere tit for tat.
Bloody the gavel, it bloodies you back.
His fault, he stuck his nose in my business.
My fault, I stuck my nose in God's business,
did not let God take vengeance by His clock.
Yes, I'm dead—meddler me bound for the bone
yard. One less Hambone, my nose my headstone.

ST. OH

We aren't actors, we're puppets. Pimp a string
we jig. Who pimps the strings? We pimp the strings.
We are the puppets and the puppeteers.
We wince and make each other dance and wince.
Got Claudius pimping my lines, me his.
Laertes and I pimping each others.
The grave-diggers pimp anybody's string.
And only Yorick's skull dares to pimp theirs.
Our pure puppet, Miss Oh, pulls no one's strings.
She's our white emptiness, St. Amnesia,
who can't decide whether she's fish or fowl:
fowl when lost at the creek, out on a limb,
fish when it breaks, and she forgets to swim.

SOMETHING ROTTEN IN NORTON'S ANTHOLOGY

This play's got poison, spooks, Italians, sword
play, grave play, bed play, play-in-play . . . madness.
Has tons of thrilla fantasy toe-cheese . . .
hot heads, cold heads, no heads, Budweiser smiles.
But boils down to—quiet talk, big yawns, rat screams.
We thespians like this Vengeance Interruptus.
We stay on stage longer. We're literature
breathing. It beats dying and lying there
deepfreezed. Can't cough. Can't itch. Achieve pure corpse.
While others wink and hoot and jaw blank verse,
until Act 5, where the play ought to start,
a gangbang swoon of poison and spilled guts,
actors doing their I'm-dying routines.
But, first, four acts of violin sniveling,
three hours of Hamwho versus Hamwho,
of tongue foreplay before the sword's unzipped.
Result? Two plays in one: Killjoy Hambo Rambo,
and Poetry Boy Hambaud Rimbaud.

OPHELIA AND GERTRUDE BIKINI THE POOL

Looks like they got on tiny tourniquets,
their milk sacks and their moss barely covered.
We at a pool? Greenhouse? Or an ER?
Some of the men poolside deserve a wreath,
so stiff they could be slid into a hearse.
They watch Gertrude sashay up to the bar.
She's young as Oh, belly flat as a snake's.
She circles back, teaching snake curvature
and slithering like machinery sex,
like screws twist when threading the nut,
like commode water circles when you flush.

QUEEN BARBIE AND KING KEN

Gertrude went to the masquerade whoopla
as Queen Barbie Doll and Claude as King Ken,
mom's breasts high as the Statue of Liberty's,
King Ken's comb-over curled from off his back.
If only mother were Queen Barbie Doll
and Claude were Ken, there'd be no tabloid trash.
Hike Barbie's dress—no crescent to airbrush.
Pull off Ken's shirt—no monkey pelt to comb,
and Ken Doll's crown only a close haircut.
But Claude's comb-over crowns our whore Kingdom;
hair-sprayed so slick, he's a walking condom.

REYNALDO LOSES HIS MARBLES

Here's how Reynaldo bought McDonald's farm.
I caught him in back of the barn with Claude,
doing x-rate. I'm crouched behind Bessie.
Were shooting marbles, these old nasty filths.
Loser would have shed his hat or pants
and chug a Bud. Wore leather thongs, big guts.
And kept shooting once they had shucked their clothes
for who'd first have to cough up his dentures.
No big surprise: Reynaldo, on his knees,
his cake hole toothless as a fresh donut.
And right there David Hume rocked me with thought.
Dave said, the world's a rat and God its soul.
Then, Claudius reared-up, revealing his
fully-tromboned music. And I gasped, "Yikes."
Four eyes swiveled. I hoped they thought Bessie
had gasped. I'm worming out of there, when Claude
assured Rey Rey I must have been a rat.
I looked back and nailed Rey Rey with a wink.
His heart said Pow . . . him a buck-naked boy,
nailed by my eye's atom. Ain't life a turd?
His mouth nor hiney covered by fig leaves.
The world's a rat, heaven's Velveeta cheese.

THE HORTICULTURE SONG

My mother is an incestuous whore,
      sing horticulture, horticulture croon,
and I'm a black cactus, a bald cactus,
a pin-cushion of needles turned inward,
      sing horticulture, horticulture drone.
If crazy is a self-impaled cactus,
then sanity's the bud that drives you nuts.
      Sing horticulture, horticulture croon.
What's Gertrude's furrow but Claude's rut?
And sanity the mom that drives you nuts.
      Drone horticulture, horticulture drone.

PRINCESS DIANA AND OPHELIA VICTORIOUS

Today we mash the brakes in memory of
our Princess Diana Cinderella,
our era's own Venus Victorious.
Or, write on your tablet, our age's Oh.
But with that said, who are they, Di and Oh?
Born not of woman, but of ad execs.
Ophelia's Sheets, from Cannon Mills.
And Cinderella Di sells magazines,
her neck long as a swan's, her smile a duck's.
We scream for Di, our ice cream from heaven,
but already our tears have washed our hands,
while Miss Oh lives painted by Delacroix
and ooh-la-la'd by all the French poets
from Mallarme and Hugo to Rimbaud.
Sure, Miss Di gets to pucker with a frog,
but Miss Oh springs from the tongue of Laforgue.

GERTRUDE NEVER WITHOUT A TAMALE LONG

My mom, with her donkey philosophy,
thinks life but a Juarez of jumping beans.
Get bucked off Bean A, whoa, straddle Bean B.
B drowns? No set back. C's cranking the yacht.
Go with the flow like the tequila worm.
I can't. My head's a cloudy aquarium.
A school of minnows picks a quarrel with me.
One says, "Cut Claude Ball's head off at his waist."
Another burps, "But don't stain your conscience."
But how? How lop a head and it not leak?
How murder but murder unmurderful?
How make a dead worm in alcohol smile?
How climb my mother's stall and not stumble,
while she shacks up and our cookie crumbles.

THREE-LEGGED GOD

The moment I punctured Polonius,
God's sword began swinging over my head,
ticking: Vengeance Is Mine Saith The Lord.
I'd been too hell-bent to walk at God's pace,
to let God drop the trap door under Claude.
Result, my neck beneath God's pendulum.
Now, there's a faceless clock—my head whacked off.
But God's the clock. God moves walking in place,
the pendulum his crutch. I made God race.

OPHELIA AND THE PANTY PROBLEM

It's her birthday. Surprise her with panties?
But thong or bucket hip? Silk or cotton?
Get Pandemoniums or Tease Pan Tease?
Which gift wrap up? It doesn't matter which.
What Oh wants is for me to scratch my head
and quiz myself—what style makes her slimmer?
Thong, or bucket, or boxer-briefs for boys.
She wants to think I cared. These, these, or these?
I'm not to see her as an exclamation mark
of Nordic grace, Nazi-sure of herself,
but as a puzzle even to herself.
Once she doesn't puzzle her life is lost.
It's mystery holds a man, not innocence,
as sure as white lies lace the wedding dress,

SWEET NOTHINGS

Men's sweet nothings are nothings for the ear.
But Ophelia's sweet nothings are no-things,
the nothing there between her legs. I ask
Oh how it feels to have nothing, except
a wound that never heals. What kinda deal
is that? She answers, I may have a gash
there, but at least my guts aren't spilling out
like yours. What deal did you work out?

GERTRUDE'S CIRCUS TAIL

What can I do? My mom's a wildcat whore,
lashing her tail like she's a sex circus?
Claws brimstone pink, eye-liner brimstone blue.
And Clawed Balls jumping through her circus hoop. Calm
down, I tell myself, we're all catnip.
But does mom's tail have to be a bullwhip?

CAN NAVY BOY DO IT?

Though it's a gold leaf-rattling autumn day,
Snow White-blue sky and sun by Goldilocks,
I drown. Fall flattens me, knocks my toupee
off my headstone, and my resolve grows bald,
though I've reason to cheer-up my shadow.
Flatman, I say, Flatman, wake up, good news:
I know the King's ready to ice me, so
bubble, bubble, I'll kill him first,
I'll go naval. I'll sink lower than him
and pull his plug, us two shit submarines
crawling in ooze, hard on each other's tail.
God steers my tub, we're breathing laughing gas,
my radar's up, my ears hum like sea shells,
torpedo aimed, but do I have the balls
to kill a king? Or like my Flatman, stall.

MOTHER LOVE GONE COUNTRY

"Mad as the sea," so says mom to cover
my fake madness. She lies to Claude easy
as hiking up her skirt. What's Claude to her?
A fool to pull the wool out from under.
He's her school-boy. And what's she teaching him?
That Grand Ole Opry tear jerk and NASCAR
Anthem, "The Cheater's Curse," which goes like this:
"Love, if she'll cheat for you, she'll cheat on you.
Love, it's all in the lingerie. You do
know, Love, enough lace and she'll hang you, too."

PIRATE FOO FOO

Casinos change us into Someone X.
At Pirate Bay we Blackbeards and Beardettes.
Or Humphrey Bogart piloting the Queen.
It's movies, now, the world no more a stage.
A free eye patch will make my ship come in.
Or, cover both eyes and double my luck.
Ophelia and I go. I lose her. No. She's up
on stage. What? Singing like a hen farmer,
grabbing her crotch and chanting nasty talk
that sounds like rap or angry cheerleading:
"The pretty pullet, just would not pull it,"
she wailed. She nuts? We're in no farm movie.
We're skulking out of there, and she sings out,
"The little pullet never did pull it.
Boys cockadoodled, lying through their beaks."
I shoved her in the Land Rover. She asked,
"So, what's the movie, Ham? Are these speed bumps
mountains? Why this four-wheel drive frat machine?
To twirl us around parking-garage switchbacks?
What's your movie, African Queen Gets Stuck?
Hambeau, you're in your movie, I'm in mine.
Love is to splice our thrillers into one.
I'm saying, Hambogart, let's make a deal.
Life isn't real, only reel after reel."

HAMBOO AND THE OEDIPUS COMPLEX APARTMENTS

When asked if I would speak on Oedipus—
why, yes, I wrote the Cliff Notes on us both,
then boiled them down to fortune-cookie blurbs:
THOSE BOYS O-REX AND HAM WERE BUT
TWO TITTY BABIES AND DADDY HATERS.
So, I'm explaining the O-Rex Complex,
while thinking some of these scholars might not
know Oedipus Complex from Apartment Complex.
One scholar says she knows Oedipus Rex
isn't kin to Tyrannosaurus Rex,
although all tyrants are tyrants, but what
if O-Rex had the T-Rex Complex first?"
Brilliant, I thought, then gave my Slacker Rex
speech. How if Oed had been a laggard slob,
he'd not have run from home because some drunk
called him a bastard. Poor Oed—too earnest,
wedgie between his cheeks, wedgie between his eyes.
The words my scholars gave him were: pervert,
asshole, mothafucka, his children's bro.
My nose-ring Plato said, "This Oedy, dumb.
This riddle-solving plague stopper, pure dumb.
Scared he would wax his dad and bang him mom,
All he needed to do? Avoid gray hair.
Break it down: go on green and stop on gray.
gray on the face or on the puddin place."
Life is simple, that's what I took away:
go down on blonde, but hit the brakes on gray.

YOURS, LOVE FOREVER DROOL

I'm blue, I'm sewage crud, and cesspool goop.
My head's on wrong until I reach the house,
and there I'm greeted by the Basset, George,
who thinks I'm his true love and has a fit:
twisting, wagging, crooning, and snuffling, while
curving his log-self into a semi-circle,
with both his North and South pointed at me,
so I can choose face, butt, or both at once,
he's my half donut. But I hold my cards.
He then flops on the floor, moaning, yelping,
and gives me all his tummy's big freckles,
his buddy money, dapples big as dimes
and quarters, my pot of gold just because
I'm his jackpot. So, how can I be puke
and slime, soiled penis cheese, in short, unloved,
when I've got George the Basset giving me
his half-a-donut love and life savings?
I can't. How whine with George licking my face
like I'm an ice cream cone on fire. Yes, dear
life makes sense even when it's robbery.
If life's a cheat, then love's the lottery.

LET MR. J. ALFRED PRUFROCK BE A LESSON

Go troll for love, Hambeau. Spank on Old Spice
and troll, my man. Don't hole up like old J.
Prufrock, safe in his kitchen, with the sink
filled up in case a mermaid might drop in.
Go troll, Hambaud. Don't sulk. Rogaine, why not?
Viagra, Lipitor, Botox. Don't mope.
Don't sputter like an outboard that won't crank:
Why Why Why Why Why am I so lonely?
Troll, dude, find out if bleached blondes are whitecaps
and drown. Or find whitecaps are platinum blondes
and swim. Or fall in love. At least find out
if her hot faucet's cold, or her cold hot.
Start with a splash maybe down at the beach.
But don't stay home and suck a Safeway peach.

THE ICEMAN HERE AND THERE, THE PANTYBLITZ

Some days life chills. My spine's an icicle
clean down into the floor, tongue an ice cube,
eyes ice marbles, my head a block of ice,
a world of ice, mirrors within mirrors.
Not so with my Mutter, who's way too cool
in TNT panties and Third Reich over-kill,
running around haltered helter skelter,
her banzai pantyblitz shrieking full blaze,
rolling up husbands in her avalanche
as full of fire as a glacier's of ice,
while I, Hammy, star of the show, stand by,
the mummy of mirrors, begging advice.

HAMLET TIGHTENS UP THE MLA

We've too many Hamlets for God to keep
the right one (me) before the lit-crit eye.
Horatio tells the world I'm Ham N Eggs,
a regular guy, like Elvis pre-Elvis.
And Fortinbras blabbers that I'm Hambo,
a soldier boy and not a panty mannequin.
And Gertrude tells the world I'm le Hambaud,
Plato's prince, poet, and philosopher.
Why do you MLA geese want a job?
The world's a goner. Dad says I'm Hamboo,
a scaredy cat, but my thumb on the nuke.

LAERTES ATE A PELICAN

Laertes, now, claims he's a pelican.
I think he's right. Look at his A-bomb mouth.
It's bigger than his head, which is his ass.
Old Sackmouth Lar Tease. Says he'll cough up blood
for any throat that's thirsty. Laertes,
what does he know of soul-eyed pelicans?
He doesn't have even a wren's bird brains.
Thinks poppycocks mate with Alfred Hitchcocks
until blue-faced from birthing shuttlecocks.
I'm who knows pelicans, the can-do bird.
The pelican's a flying plumbing store
of bends and tailouts, crashes like a sink
into the bay. Blue-collar bird, your pelican:
lunch-sack mouth, beer belly, and skinny legs.
Bird of the working-woman, too—wing span
covers your Sunday table, and his feet
two platters he sets down and serves himself.
Laertes is no more a pelican
than a commode is an amphibian.

THE PLAY'S SWEET 400th

The play's 400th birthday cake comes soon,
and I've blimped-up bigger than late Elvis.
I, too, when on the pot, can't see my cods,
my paunch a big chicken-white hairy purse.
But I'd big cods in the 17th Century—
my codpiece a fur pot. People swoon-talked.
There goes Hambo the Great. There goes Hambone
the Bad: stabs you, then shakes your hand, then drags
you where noses will stare under the stairs.
But now as the 20th Century fizzles,
I've gone hemorphoditic apocalyptic,
per femme crits and le deconstructionists.
One says I'm Hambelle, one says I'm sliced ham.
No, I'm Fatboy Elvis, a hunka burning spam.
Yes, I don't like the bloke I am, either.
You stare because I'm your mirror.

OH QUEENLY TO THE LAKE

Christmas parade, Miss Oh went as Queen Claus
and threw a fit, on top the top-down Benz.
She might have thrown kisses or puppet-waved.
But she flung CD's like death-edged Frisbees.
First, flung HOLE at Gertrude, "Your majesty,
here's one a girl can't have too many of."
Sailed-out at Claudius her 9 INCH NAILS,
as if to say: Lie down on this, fakir,
then still staring at Claudius, she sang,
"Don't throw away my love on an old flame.
Her whiskey lips will wash out in the rain.
Her love is as false as her eyelashes.
She wears so much make-up her face clashes."
At me Miss Oh chunked FRANK ZAPPA'S MOTHER.
Oh thinks I have a hard leg for Gertrude.
Oh screamed at me in Country-Western twang:
"Your mom paints herself like a totem pole,
but whitewash can't make young face that old."
Then, her white Nazi box eased off the brakes,
rounded the curve, and headed for the lake.

CHRISTMAS SHOPPING EASY

At 3-Toed Ty's upscale Muzak headshop,
I looked for Claudius a sailor cap.
The music sucked that way—Jimmy Buffet
thumping one-hundred and one coconuts.
But one-hundred and one Michael Jackson's
hiccupped me toward Walk Backwards Gangsta Pop.
White glove? Got it, in spite of no owner manual.
I'd replace the sequins with crushed razors
for Claudius' frequent penis checks.
Or has he scratched himself a cleft down there?
A bleeding boy. Now, I won't have to kill
him. He can give himself that thrill.

SKULL TURTLES INTERRUPTUS

Here's how Laertes shines his red brightest.
We're at Dog Yaughan's Pool Hall to watch
the winter solstice Running of the Skulls.
The skulls are turtles with skulls painted on
their backs, on top of which a candle burns.
These lighted skulls sit in the middle of
a circle made out of longneck empties.
The gamblers calm down, and the lights flick off.
First speedster through the bottles wins.
Racers include Blob, Moving Van the Third,
Earlene's Lawn Mower, Bimbo Tank, and such.
They were slipping in gear when Laertes
let go his armadillo in their midst.
Yaughan's Pool Hall blew straight up. Ophelia screamed,
and Osric hopped hen-like onto a table top.
The lights snapped on, Yaughan kicked out Laertes
and his army and re-started the race.
Half-inch from winning, Bimbo Tank clamped shy,
allowing Earlene's Mower to plow through,
her candle sputtering like a sparkler.
And where was our merry Larry? Larry
sulked outside with an unlit cigarette,
mad he had no light, or mad at the night.
No problem. He's a moth. He'll find the light.

OPHELIA SWANS HER LADYSHIP

Her swan-ness was her mystery, her X.
We loved Oh for magic algebra,
her riddle of gliding from A to B
without effort, the same way white is white,
but isn't, is all of the rainbow's tints.
Ophelia's presence was this same absence.
When she bobbed downstream on her petticoat
and swan-like studied her reflection when
it rose up to embrace her, what could she
do but embrace it back? It was herself,
this reflection, this was her emptiness.
Now, she'd see what was in it for herself.

NEW YEAR'S EVE AT THE TIT FOR TAT

A tattoo shop. I got a portrait of
Oh seen from overhead, her on her hands
and knees, presenting doggy style
in such a way, by sleight-of-eye,
she also presented the male package:
her back a blonde penis,
her flared buttocks two blue gonads.
How better show she got the royal shaft,
sailing off in her petticoat life-raft?

ZEN WART

Was at Ophelia's grave to do my Zen
memorial—to stand as her headstone,
a breathing nullity. And who showed up
and ignored my long, black funeral face?
Laertes, and with his ukulele,
which he tried to play Southern Gothic style,
as mock fiddle, with car-antenna bow,
hair snake-oil combed. He squalled, oh Lord,
about sadness, about the Smoky Mountains Oh
had dropped on him. On me she'd slapped a wart,
I guess, my sadness just a rash, I guess.
Laertes, fresh from his coop of Parisian chicks,
what would he know about lock-jaw sadness?
What know about screeching a mock fiddle?
Have ringworms taught him don't give women rings?
Have washer-wringer Maytags rusted out his crotch?
Laertes with his Smokies of sadness,
they're nothing—zits. Scrape zits off with a cheese
grater. But my whole life's a seeping wart.
Scrape off and grows back worse than Modern Art.

FORTINBONE AND HAMBONE XYLOPHONE

Goodbye Denmark, I raise my bloody hand
for Fortinbras. Long may he do nothing,
the vulture kid, who let us kill ourselves.
All he did was obey his gray uncle,
"Pickers off Denmark." Fortinbras obeyed
and let slothful patience ripen our stink.
Laertes and I obeyed no gray heads.
Result? Death wrote new poems in our graveyard.
Well, Fortinbras the Patient gets my vote.
My problem was I played too many parts,
tinked my silver tongues like a xylophone,
while Fortinbras the Patient Dumb-De-Dumb
cooked our goose while he let the cows come home.
He gets the last plink of my xylophone.

FORTINBRAS FROM AIR FORCE ONE, FIRST SOLILOQUY

I'm riding shotgun, and the sky's dire gray.
I smell poot-salad nuclear sulphur.
The sky chicken has dropped the rotten egg,
rr maybe not. Or what? Do I say Fe Fi Fo
and drop the bomb? Or Meany Miney Mo
and pass the chicken. What's my TV say?
The soaps say, KNOCK EM UP. The psycho shows say,
KN0CK EM UP, FIRST, AND THEN KNOCK EM OUT.
I call London. London is out to lunch.
I scratch my brow, picking a safe that has
no lock. I'm calling Italy—Leonardo,
this here our last supper or what? Are we
under attack? I drop the last mushroom
on everybody's plate? Or what? I wait?
Is Big Ben slicing life's last piece of cake?